T0044436

TO:

FROM:

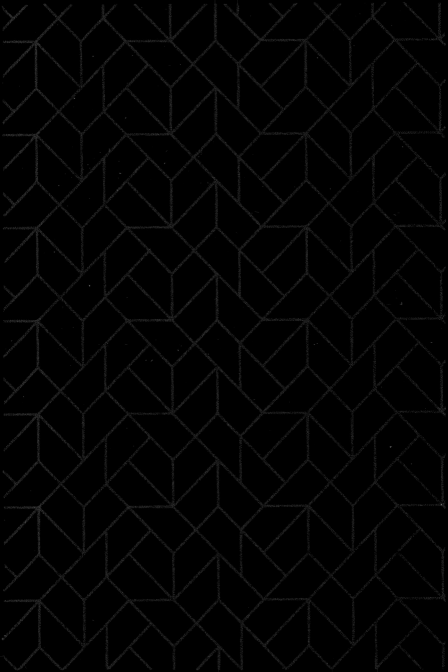

LESSONS ON
SUCCESS

17 Principles of
Personal Achievement
Through Action & Attitude

NAPOLEON HILL

Published by Simple Truths, an imprint of Sourcebooks
P.O. Box 4410, Naperville, Illinois 60567-4410
(630) 961-3900
sourcebooks.com

Printed and bound in China.
OGP 10 9 8 7 6 5 4 3 2 1

Whatever the mind can conceive
and believe, it can achieve.

—NAPOLEON HILL

CONTENTS

Before success comes in any man's life, he's sure to meet with much temporary defeat and perhaps some failures. When defeat overtakes a man, the easiest and the most logical thing to do is to quit. That's exactly what the majority of men do.

—NAPOLEON HILL

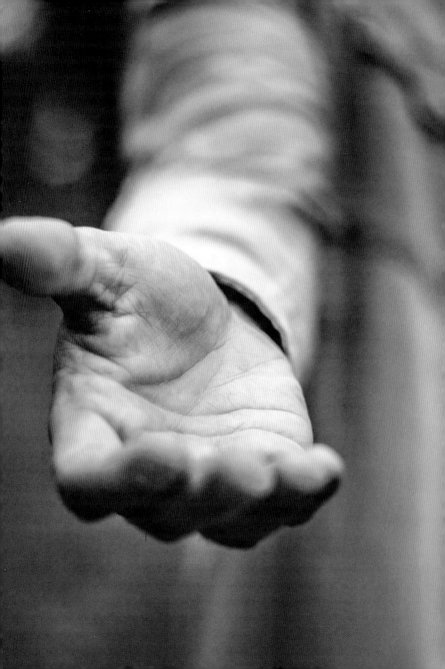

FOREWORD

It has always been my belief that a
man should do his best, regardless of
how much he receives for his services
or the number of people he may be
serving or the class of people served.

—NAPOLEON HILL

IN MY POSITION AS EXECUTIVE director of the Napoleon Hill
Foundation, I have often been asked, "Why should a
person need more than one good book on success?"
The answer to that question can be shown by recall-
ing our early learning. We were taught our ABCs by

repeating them through games and stories or simply reciting them until they became a part of our memory. For example, each of us probably learned our multiplication tables in the same manner. Each set of numbers was repeated so many times that if asked what eight times eight equals, the answer sixty-four would be recalled with very little effort. Another excellent reason to continue exposure to inspirational material, whether it be a self-help magazine, book, audio, video, or seminar, is to be among the estimated 5 percent who are truly successful.

You will likely discover that your desires will change markedly as you advance in years. As a young person, it is normal to be concerned with accomplishments to provide housing, education, and everyday needs and wants. Most of your efforts are directed at obtaining security. Though you will no doubt contribute to your church or favorite charities, they will not be your primary focus.

While the principles of success philosophy do not

change, it will become evident that your desire to make a difference does. It will become normal to put more energy to helping those in the world who are less fortunate.

Napoleon Hill knew the keys to success and shared that wisdom with millions. As you read the following pages, you'll discover the principles you need to follow to be among the truly successful and discover ways that application in your life will help you reach your goals.

In the final analysis, all successful people will be remembered more for what they gave rather than what they got in life.

Don M. Green

Executive Director

Napoleon Hill Foundation

INTRODUCTION

The ladder of success
is never crowded at the top.
—NAPOLEON HILL

OVER ONE HUNDRED YEARS AGO, a fortuitous meeting in Pittsburgh completely changed the life of one young man and ushered in a new philosophy of personal achievement that has served as the foundation of the success movement for the last century.

That young man was Napoleon Hill, a young reporter from Virginia. That meeting in the fall of 1908 was, as he described it, when "the hand of destiny reached out."

Hill had been granted an interview with Andrew Carnegie, the steel magnate who was then the world's richest man. Hill dove into the questioning, asking, "Mr. Carnegie, to what do you attribute your phenomenal success?"

The industrialist, then seventy-three, opened up quickly and, with wit and his unrivaled gift for anecdote, began to relate the stories of his achievements. Hill could hardly keep up his shorthand notes when Carnegie then began to expound on his and others' theories of personal achievement.

Carnegie lamented, "It's a shame that each new generation must find the way to success by trial and error when the principles really are clear-cut."

On the third day of the interview, Carnegie offered him the opportunity to organize the world's first practical philosophy of individual achievement. "I will introduce you to men who can and will collaborate with you in its organization. Do you want the opportunity, and will you follow through if it is given to you?"

Hill blurted out with characteristic enthusiasm, "Yes! I'll undertake the job, and I'll finish it."

Carnegie withdrew a stopwatch and told Hill it had taken him exactly twenty-nine seconds to respond. Carnegie told him, "The offer would have been withdrawn after sixty seconds. It has been my experience that a man who cannot reach a decision promptly cannot be depended on to carry through any decision he may make. I have also discovered that most who reach decisions promptly usually have the capacity to move with definiteness of purpose in other circumstances.

"Very well," said Carnegie. "You have one of the two important qualities that will be needed by the man who organizes the philosophy I have described. Now I will learn whether or not you have the second. If I give you this opportunity, are you willing to devote twenty years of your time to research the causes of success and failure without pay, earning your own living as you go along?"

Hill was stunned. He had assumed that Carnegie would subsidize him from his enormous fortune.

"It is not unwillingness to supply the money," Carnegie explained. "It is my desire to know if you have in you the natural capacity to go the extra mile, that is, to render service before trying to collect for it."

Napoleon Hill met Carnegie's second test. He would go on to write the American philosophy of personal achievement.

For the next twenty years, Hill would interview such men as Thomas Edison, Henry Ford, Alexander Graham Bell, King Gillette, Theodore Roosevelt, John Rockefeller, and others. In 1928, he published *The Law of Success*, a compilation of success secrets from the greatest achievers of that time that, for the first time in the history of the world, revealed the true philosophy upon which all personal success is built.

From those teachings would come, nine years later, *Think and Grow Rich*, considered by many to be the greatest success book of all time. It offered essential principles for improving one's health, wealth, and success. While readers today will note that the language of the book reflects mid-twentieth-century America, the principles expounded on for a successful life remain as powerful and pertinent today as they did more than eighty years ago.

This gift book offers Napoleon Hill's seventeen principles of personal achievement in an easy-to-read format so you can easily learn them and start applying them to your life today. Remember, if you conceive it and believe it, you can achieve it!

DEFINITENESS OF PURPOSE

Whatever the mind can conceive and believe, it can achieve with positive mental attitude.

—NAPOLEON HILL

DON'T BE LIKE A SHIP without a rudder, powerless and directionless.

Definiteness of purpose is the starting point of all achievement. All individual achievement begins with the adoption of a definite major purpose and a specific plan for its attainment. Without a purpose and a plan, people drift aimlessly through life.

Ideas form the foundation of all fortunes and the starting point of all inventions. Once you learn how to harness the power of your mind and then how to organize the knowledge, you begin to keep your mind on the things you want and off the things you do not want.

DEVELOP A DEFINITENESS OF PURPOSE

- You should have one high, desirable, outstanding goal and keep it ever before you.
- Determine and fix in your mind exactly what you desire.
- Evaluate and determine exactly what you will give in return.
- Set a definite date for exactly when you intend to possess your desire.
- Clearly define your plan for achievement. Write out precisely and concisely exactly what you want, exactly when you want to achieve it, and exactly what you intend to give in return.

- Each and every day, morning and evening, read your written statement aloud.

Your ship will not come in unless you have first sent one out. Be sure about what you want from life and doubly sure of what you have to give in return. You will get exactly and only what you ask and work for.

KEY TAKEAWAYS

1. What ideas and plans are in your mind, awaiting attention and focus from you, that could bring you happiness and success?

2. How can you use the pillars of focus and purpose to drive these ideas forward?

3. By using the guide outlined above and defining yourself for achievement, you can find success. Have you attempted to do so and find you are still not hitting your stride? Pick another idea or goal from your mind, and try these exercises again. You'll need your heart and mind to be aligned in order to achieve.

MASTERMIND ALLIANCE

We are the masters of our fate,
the captains of our souls, because we
have the power to control our thoughts.

—NAPOLEON HILL

NO MAN CAN BECOME A permanent success without taking others along with him.

The mastermind principle consists of an alliance of two or more minds working in perfect harmony for the attainment of a common definite objective. Success does not come without the cooperation of others.

An active alliance of two or more minds, in a spirit

of perfect harmony, stimulates each mind to a higher degree of courage than that ordinarily experienced and paves the way for the state of mind known as faith.

ESTABLISH A MASTERMIND ALLIANCE

- Your mastermind alliance can be created by surrounding yourself or aligning yourself with the advice, counsel, and personal cooperation of several people who are willing to lend you their wholehearted aid for the attainment of your objective.
- You can create a mastermind alliance with your spouse, friend, or coworker. Once a mastermind alliance is formed, the group must become and remain active. The group must move in a definite plan, at a definite time, toward a definite common objective.

The first step toward a successful mastermind alliance is to get on good terms with yourself.

KEY TAKEAWAYS

1. How can you unblock your mind and enter into good terms with yourself? What is holding you back from truly supporting yourself and your ideas as you would a friend or loved one?

2. When identifying an alliance for yourself, who immediately comes to mind? As noted, a friend, spouse, or coworker would each make a great partner as you proceed, but taking a moment to listen to your immediate instinct for who would align with your goals and thinking through who can really pull success from you is an exercise worth doing.

3. Once you have formed an alliance between yourself and one or more others, what are some tactics you can use to hold everyone accountable?

APPLIED FAITH

Great achievement is usually born of great sacrifice and is never the result of selfishness.

—NAPOLEON HILL

FAITH IS AN ACTIVE STATE of mind.

Faith is a state of mind through which your aims, desires, plans, and purposes may be translated into their physical or financial equivalent.

Applied faith means action, specifically the habit of applying your faith under any and all circumstances. It is faith in your God, yourself, your fellow being, and the unlimited opportunities available to you.

Faith without action is dead.

Faith is the art of believing by doing.

USE APPLIED FAITH

- Applied faith is belief in an objective or purpose backed by unqualified activity. If you want results, try a prayer. When you pray, you express your gratitude and thanksgiving for the blessing you already have received.
- Affirm the objectives of your desires through prayer each night and morning. Inspire your imagination to see yourself already in possession of them.
- Prayer is your greatest power!

Faith removes limitations. Close the door to fear behind you, and see how quickly the door to faith will open in front of you.

If you don't believe it yourself, don't ask anyone else to do so.

KEY TAKEAWAYS

1. When you hit roadblocks, where do you turn?
    Most of us turn inward and berate ourselves
    for failures big and small. What could happen
    if you instead turned to a higher power?
    Or instead of turning inward with negative
    energy, what if you had faith in yourself and
    turned inward with thoughts of changing
    roadblocks into solutions?

2. How can you continue to bolster your
    self-esteem?

3. When you do take a moment for prayer or
    reflection, what fruits are you able to yield?

GOING THE EXTRA MILE

Most people have achieved their greatest success just one step beyond their greatest failure.

—NAPOLEON HILL

PUT YOUR MIND TO WORK. Access your ability and energy.

Going the extra mile is the action of rendering more and better service than that for which you are presently paid. When you go the extra mile, the law of compensation comes into play. This universal law neither permits any living thing to get something for nothing nor allows any form of labor to go unrewarded.

You will find that Mother Nature goes the extra mile in everything that she does. She does not create just barely enough of each gene or species to get by; she produces an overabundance to take care of all emergencies that arise and still have enough left to guarantee the perpetuation of each form of life.

GO THE EXTRA MILE

- Render more and better service for which you are paid, and do it with a positive mental attitude. Form the habit of going the extra mile because of the pleasure you get out of it and because of what it does to you and for you deep down inside.
- It is inevitable that every seed of useful service you sow will multiply itself and come back to you in overwhelming abundance.

Start going the extra mile, and opportunity will follow you.

KEY TAKEAWAYS

1. How can you align your goals with those of service? How can you ensure your goals are ones that deliver more than even you originally intended?

2. How can you use your goals and actions to drive others forward?

3. What can you do today to push yourself further than others expect of you? Than you expect of yourself?

PLEASING PERSONALITY

The world has the habit of making room for the man whose actions show that he knows where he is going.

—NAPOLEON HILL

THE ATTITUDE YOU TRANSMIT TO others will tell more about you than the words you say or how you look.

Your personality is your greatest asset or your greatest liability, for it embraces everything that you control: mind, body, and soul. A person's personality is the person. It shapes the nature of your thoughts, your deeds, your relationships with others, and it establishes the boundaries of the space you occupy in the world.

Personality is the sum total of one's mental, spiritual, and physical traits and habits that distinguish one from all others. It is the factor that determines whether one is liked or disliked by others.

ASSEMBLE AN ATTRACTIVE PERSONALITY

- It is imperative that you develop the habit of being sensitive to your own reactions to individuals, circumstances, and events and to the reactions of individuals and groups to what you say, think, or do.

- Positive factors of a pleasing personality include

tolerance, common courtesy, alertness, tactfulness, personal magnetism, sportsmanship, sincerity, sense of humor, and patience.

What you believe yourself to be, you are. Your mental attitude is the most dependable key to your personality. A smiling face often defeats the cruelest of antagonists.

KEY TAKEAWAYS

1. If you aren't proud of the person you see in the mirror every day, what do you need to do to change? How can you either shift the image or reflect the aspects of yourself you are proud of?

2. Looking inward, what pieces of you are you ashamed of? Afraid of? How can you come to love or change these aspects of yourself and move to acceptance?

3. A positive attitude changes all things. How can you bring positivity forward in all aspects of your life?

PERSONAL INITIATIVE

Create a definite plan for carrying
out your desire and begin at once,
whether you are ready or not,
to put this plan into action.

—NAPOLEON HILL

PERSONAL INITIATIVE IS THE DYNAMO that spurs the faculty of
your imagination into action.

"There are two types of men," said Andrew Carnegie,
"who never amount to anything. One is the fellow who
never does anything except that which he is told to do.
The other is the fellow who never does more than he

is told to do. The man who gets ahead does the thing that should be done without being told to do it."

Personal initiative is the inner power that starts all action. It is the power that inspires the completion of that which one begins.

It is, in fact, self-motivation. Motivation is that which induces action or determines choice.

CREATE PERSONAL INITIATIVE

- A motive is that inner urge only within the individual that incites you to action, such as an idea, an emotion, a desire, or an impulse. It is a hope or other force that starts in an attempt to produce specific results.
- Motivate yourself with a positive mental attitude. Hope is the magic ingredient in motivation, but the secret of accomplishment is getting into action.
- Use and develop the self-starter!

Successful people move on their own initiative, and they know where they are going before they start.

KEY TAKEAWAYS

1. What are you putting off to tomorrow that you can instead take on today?

2. When you're low on motivation, what actions help you personally cultivate the positive mental attitude you'll need to achieve?

3. What do you need to start driving forward not just those goals tasked to you but your own goals, today?

POSITIVE MENTAL ATTITUDE

Every adversity, every failure, every heartache carries with it the seed of an equal or greater benefit.

—NAPOLEON HILL

A POSITIVE MENTAL ATTITUDE IS the greatest of life's riches.

A positive mental attitude is the right, honest, constructive thought, action, or reaction to any person, situation, or set of circumstances.

It allows you to build on hope and overcome the negative attitudes of despair and discouragement. It gives you the mental power, the feeling, the confidence to do anything you make your mind up to do. It is the "I can...I will" attitude applicable to all circumstances in your life.

A positive mental attitude is the catalyst necessary for achieving worthwhile success.

BUILD A POSITIVE MENTAL ATTITUDE

- Create and maintain a positive mental attitude through your own willpower, based on motives of your own adaption.
- Be sensitive to your own reactions by controlling your emotional responses. Believe that any goal can be achieved. Develop right habits of thought and action.
- Maintain the right attitude—a positive mental attitude.

A positive mental attitude is an irresistible force that knows no such thing as an immovable object. A positive mind finds a way it can be done; a negative mind looks for all the ways it can't be done. Change your mental attitude, and the world around you will change accordingly.

KEY TAKEAWAYS

1. We're all plagued by negative thinking. How can you shift your mindset to one of positivity (finding paths forward, looking for opportunities, etc.) as opposed to negativity (focusing on the bad results first, not solutions)?

2. When your plan comes to a halt, how can you overcome without an emotional response?

3. How can you make your first instincts ones of positivity?

ENTHUSIASM

The jack-of-all-trades seldom is good at any. Concentrate all of your efforts on one definite chief aim.

—NAPOLEON HILL

ENTHUSIASM INSPIRES ACTION AND IS the most contagious of all emotions.

Enthusiasm is faith in action. It is the intense emotion known as burning desire. It comes from within, although it radiates outwardly in the expression of one's voice and countenance.

Enthusiasm is power because it is the instrument

by which adversities and failures and temporary defeats may be transmuted into action backed by faith. The flame of enthusiasm burning within you turns thought into action.

CONTROL YOUR ENTHUSIASM

- To become enthusiastic about achieving a desirable goal, keep your mind on that goal day after day. The more worthy and desirable your objectives, the more dedicated and enthusiastic you will become.
- Enthusiasm thrives on a positive mind and positive action. The key to controlling your enthusiasm: always give it a worthy goal to focus on, and once you have channeled it toward a goal, it will carry you forward.

Enthusiasm starts the wheels of imagination turning.

KEY TAKEAWAYS

1. If you're not in love with your goal, why are you pursuing it?

2. If you've fallen out of love with your goal as it has become harder to achieve, how can you recapture the magic of when you started?

3. Enthusiasm is controlled by positive thinking. How can you continue using the methods you put into action from lesson 7 to drive forward with positivity, even when enthusiasm wanes?

SELF-DISCIPLINE

Life is a checkerboard, and the player opposite you is time. If you hesitate before moving, or neglect to move promptly, your men will be wiped off the board by time. You are playing against a partner who will not tolerate indecision!

—NAPOLEON HILL

IF YOU DIRECT YOUR THOUGHTS and control your emotions, you will ordain your destiny.

Self-discipline begins with the mastery of thoughts. If you do not control your thoughts, you cannot control your needs. Self-discipline calls for a balancing of the emotions of your heart with the reasoning faculty of your head.

Self-discipline is the bottleneck through which all of your personal power for success must flow. We have the power of self-determination, the ability to choose what our thoughts and actions will be.

ENFORCE SELF-DISCIPLINE

- Self-discipline is perhaps the most important function in aiding an individual in the development and maintenance of habits. Self-discipline enables a person to fix his or her entire attention upon any desired purpose and hold it there until that purpose has been attained.

- If you do not control your thoughts, you do not control your deeds. Think first and act afterward. Self-discipline is the principle by which you may voluntarily shape the patterns of your thoughts to harmonize with your goals and purposes.

Self-discipline, or self-control, means taking posses-sion of your own mind. Before trying to master others, be sure you are the master of yourself. Self-discipline is the first rule of all successful leadership.

KEY TAKEAWAYS

1. As self-discipline is the first step toward leadership, what aspects from leaders in your life can you work toward instilling in yourself?

2. Taking the previous lessons to heart, how can you control your thoughts and actions to drive forward with positivity *only*?

3. What negative habits or negative thoughts are preventing you from having full control of your life?

ACCURATE THINKING

All achievements, all earned riches,
have their beginning in an idea.

—NAPOLEON HILL

TRUTH WILL BE TRUTH, REGARDLESS of a closed mind, ignorance, or the refusal to believe.

The power of thought is the most dangerous or the most beneficial power available, depending on how it is used. Through the power of thought, man builds great empires of civilization.

Accurate thinking is based on **two** major fundamentals: inductive reasoning, based on the assumption of unknown facts and hypotheses; and deductive reasoning, based on known facts or what are believed to be facts.

THINK ACCURATELY

- You can learn from your own experiences as well as those of others when you learn how to recognize, relate, assimilate, and apply principles in order to achieve your goals.
- Learn to separate facts from fiction or hearsay evidence. Learn to separate facts into classes—important and unimportant.
- Be careful of others' opinions. They could be dangerous and destructive. Make sure your opinions are not someone else's prejudices.

Accurate thinkers permit no one to do their thinking for them.

KEY TAKEAWAYS

1. What truths are you not facing in the name of your goals? Be vulnerable and honest with yourself. Some of your greatest obstacles may only be difficult to overcome due to your own blind spots.

2. Who can you trust in your life to be honest with you? Seek their guidance. (Note, the individual or individuals you identified in lesson 2 should be able to support you!)

3. Are you too easily influenced by others? Stop and think about how others talk about your goals versus how you talk about your goals. Is there a gap you need to identify and close?

LESSON 11
CONTROLLED ATTENTION

Peace within one's mind is not a matter of luck but is a priceless possession, which can be attained only by self-discipline based upon controlled attention.

—NAPOLEON HILL

KEEP YOUR MIND ON THE things you want and off the things you don't want.

Controlled attention is organized mind power. It is the highest form of self-discipline. It is the act of coordinating all the faculties of the mind and directing their combined power to a given end or definite objective.

Controlled attention leads to a mastery in any type of human endeavor because it enables one to focus the powers of the mind upon the attainment of a definite objective and to keep it so directed at will. Great achievements come from minds that are at peace with themselves.

CONTROL YOUR ATTENTION

- When you voluntarily fix your attention upon a definite major purpose of a positive nature and force your mind through your daily habits of thought to dwell on the subject, you condition your subconscious mind to act on that purpose.

- The person who controls his or her own mind may control everything else. Keep your mind busy with thought material that may be helpful in attaining the object of your desire.

Control your own mind, and you may never be controlled by the mind of another. Riches begin with thoughts. Thinking your way through your problems is safer than wishing your way through them.

KEY TAKEAWAYS

1. When you feel your thoughts and feelings overwhelming you, all actions will suddenly shift to chaos. How do you control your attention to focus on the tasks at hand? What specific methods work for you when you feel overwhelmed?

2. In modern society, attention is hard to spare! How do screens, technology, and an "always on" culture impact your thinking? How can you ensure you are in full control of your thinking despite such distractions?

3. Instead of wishing for solutions, how can you drive them forward with actions and thoughts?

TEAMWORK

It is literally true that you can succeed best and quickest by helping others to succeed.

—NAPOLEON HILL

TEAMWORK COSTS SO LITTLE IN time and effort and pays huge dividends.

Teamwork is harmonious cooperation that is willing, voluntary, and free. Whenever the spirit of teamwork is the dominating influence in business or industry, success is inevitable. Harmonious cooperation is a priceless asset that you can acquire in proportion to your giving.

Teamwork, in a spirit of friendliness, costs little in the way of time and effort. Generosity, fair treatment, courtesy, and a willingness to serve are qualities that pay high dividends whenever they are applied in human relations.

INSPIRE TEAMWORK

- Teamwork produces power. The power produced by teamwork made by willing cooperation will endure as long as that spirit of willingness prevails.
- Teamwork builds individuals and businesses and provides unlimited opportunity for all.
- That which you share will multiply; that which you withhold will diminish.

Teamwork is sharing a part of what you have—a part that is good—with others.

KEY TAKEAWAYS

1. What do you bring to your team? If you're underdelivering, what can you begin to bring forward starting *now*?

2. What do your best teammates provide to the group? Can you adapt your own behavior to contribute at the same scale? How can you help each other?

3. How can you recruit your team to help you achieve your individual goals? How can you support teammates with their own goals?

ADVERSITY AND DEFEAT

When defeat comes, accept it as a signal that your plans are not sound, rebuild those plans, and set sail once more toward your coveted goal.

—NAPOLEON HILL

EVERY ADVERSITY YOU MEET CARRIES with it a seed of equivalent or greater benefit.

Defeat may be a stepping-stone or a stumbling block according to your mental attitude and how you relate to it yourself. It is never the same as failure unless and until it has been accepted as such.

Many so-called failures represent only a temporary defeat that may prove to be a blessing in disguise.

Your mental attitude in respect to defeat is the factor of major importance that determines whether you rise with the tides of fortune or misfortune.

LEARN FROM ADVERSITY AND DEFEAT

- Individual success usually is in exact proportion to the scope of the defeat the individual has experienced and mastered.
- Remember, the worst that can happen to you may be the best thing that can happen to you if you don't let it get the best of you.

Learn to use the winds of adversity to sail your ship of life. Close the door of your mind on all failure. If you accept defeat as an inspiration to try again with renewed confidence and determination, attaining success will only be a matter of time.

KEY TAKEAWAYS

1. If you never fail, you will never find success. How can you seek out opportunities to try, understanding this defeat will drive you forward?

2. What goals are you avoiding due to fear of failure?

3. What are you afraid of in the face of failure? How can you change your fears into actions you are eager to experience in the name of success?

CREATIVE VISION

Through some strange and powerful principle of mental chemistry that she has never divulged, nature wraps up in the impulse of strong desire something that recognizes no such word as impossible and accepts no such reality as failure.

—NAPOLEON HILL

ONLY AN OPEN MIND CAN grow.

Our greatest gift is our thinking mind. It analyzes, compares, chooses. It creates, visualizes, foresees, and generates ideas. Imagination is your mind's exercise, challenge, and adventure. It is the key to all a person's achievements, the mainspring of all human endeavor, the secret door to the soul of a person.

Creative vision may be an inborn quality of mind or an acquired quality, for it may be developed by the free and fearless use of the faculty of imagination.

CULTIVATE CREATIVE VISION

- One of the ways to increase your flow of ideas is by developing the habit of taking study time, thinking time, and planning time.
- Be quiet and motionless, and listen for that small, still voice that speaks from within you. Contemplate the ways in which you can achieve your objectives.

Imagination is the workshop of the soul wherein all plans are shaped for individual achievement.

KEY TAKEAWAYS

1. What about your goals, plans, and dreams is unique? How can you push yourself further? How big can you dream?

2. How can you create moments of quiet in order to hear that inner voice that will help you truly align to your objectives?

3. If you were completely unbound by limitations, what might you be able to achieve? Imagine your goals without limits.

HEALTH

Eat right, think right, sleep right,
and play right, and you can save
the doctor's bill for your vacation.

—NAPOLEON HILL

SOUND PHYSICAL HEALTH IS DEPENDENT upon a positive mental attitude.

You are a mind with a body. Inasmuch as your brain controls your body, recognize that sound physical health demands a positive mental attitude, a health consciousness.

To maintain a health consciousness, one must think

in terms of sound health, not in terms of illness and disease. Remember, what your mind focuses upon, your mind brings into existence.

MAINTAIN SOUND HEALTH

- To maintain a positive attitude for the development and maintenance of a sound health consciousness, use self-discipline, keep your mind free of negative thoughts and influence, and create and maintain a well-balanced life.
- Follow work with play, mental effort with physical effort, and seriousness with humor, and you will be on the road to good health and happiness.

Whatever affects the body will affect the mind; whatever affects the mind will affect the body. Don't try to cure a headache. It's better to cure the thing that caused it.

KEY TAKEAWAYS

1. What is preventing your mental health from truly flourishing?

2. Are you ignoring any physical health issues? How can you help your body reflect the health of your mind?

3. Health, in mind, body, or spirit, is always easier to maintain with support. Who can hold you accountable in regard to your health? It may be different individuals for each aspect of your health (mind, body, spirit)!

LESSON 16

BUDGETING TIME AND MONEY

More gold has been mined from the thoughts of men than has been taken from the earth.

—NAPOLEON HILL

THE SUCCESSFUL PERSON BUDGETS TIME, income, and expenditures, living within his means.

Time and money are precious resources, and few people striving for success ever believe they possess either one in excess. Understanding how you use them is an important part of evaluating your progress toward success and analyzing what may be holding you back.

Learn to budget your time to the important tasks and your money to those things related to your definite purpose.

BUDGET YOUR TIME AND MONEY

- Intelligently balance your use of time and resources, both business and personal. Take inventory of yourself and your activities so that you discover where and how you are spending your time and your money.
- Don't waste your time or your money. Ten percent of all you earn is yours to keep and invest. Like any good business, budget your money, and use your time wisely toward the attainment of your objectives.

Failures squander time and income with contemptuous disregard for their value.

KEY TAKEAWAYS

1. Where does most of your time go? Look at the inventory you made. How can you better spend your time to drive your goals?

2. Where does most of your money go? Looking at your inventory, what shifts can help you make the most of your funds?

3. There is always a balance between work and play, between saving for tomorrow and spending/investing in today. How can you ensure you are providing balance and both nurturing your now and planning for your future? Your immediate instinct may be to save and plan—after all, this is a disciplined act—but you also need to focus on your present!

HABITS

When your desires are strong
enough, you will appear to possess
superhuman powers to achieve.

—NAPOLEON HILL

YOU ARE WHERE YOU ARE and what you are because of your established habits, thoughts, and deeds.

All of us are ruled by habits. They are fastened upon us by repeated thoughts and experiences. We create patterns of thought by repeating certain ideas or behaviors and making them permanent.

Some habits are good, and some are bad. Many we

are aware of, but some we are blinded to. Each habit begins in the mind, consciously or subconsciously. Each can be developed and neutralized or changed at will through the proper use of your mind.

CREATE GOOD HABITS

- It takes a habit to replace a habit.
- Develop positive habits that will be in harmony with the achievement of your definite purpose or goal.
- Sow an act, reap a habit. Sow a habit, reap a character. Sow a character, reap a destiny.

One bad habit often spoils a dozen good ones. Only man has been given the privilege and the means to fix his own habits. You are ruled by your habits— good or bad.

KEY TAKEAWAYS

1. As your final lesson, how can you take all you have learned throughout this work and establish good, lasting habits for yourself?

2. Which habits are you most in need of cultivating? Which habits do you feel you already have that work for you? Can similar tactics apply to those where you struggle?

3. What are your habits currently sowing for you to reap? How can you shift and harvest success?

ABOUT
NAPOLEON HILL

NAPOLEON HILL WAS A PIONEER in the study of the American philosophy of personal achievement and is considered the founder of the modern genre of personal success literature. The success formulas he developed through his research have helped millions of people throughout the world achieve outstanding results in every aspect of life.

Hill was born on October 26, 1883, in a two-room log cabin in the mountains of Wise County, Virginia, a region marked by illiteracy and grinding poverty. An unruly child who idolized Jesse James, his life was transformed by his stepmother's suggestion that he put his keen imagination and initiative to use as a writer. At age fifteen, he completed grade school and began to work part-time as a mountain reporter for local, small-town newspapers, then as a reporter for *Bob Taylor's Magazine*, interviewing and writing success profiles of famous individuals.

In 1908, while on assignment, Hill met Pittsburgh industrialist Andrew Carnegie, then the richest man in the world. That meeting and Hill's almost twenty years of subsequent research that was suggested and informally sponsored by Carnegie led to the publication of *The Law of Success*, which shared the ideas and philosophy gleaned from the research. The book won wide acclaim and established Hill as a leader in the success movement. In 1937, *Think and Grow Rich* provided readers with the steps for forming a philosophy of personal achievement.

Hill's popularity led to him becoming an informal advisor to two U.S. presidents—Woodrow Wilson and Franklin D. Roosevelt. He went on to author more than thirty books, including *Success through a Positive Mental Attitude*, written with W. Clement Stone. Hill was a fixture on the motivational lecture circuit and a prolific creator of textbooks, study guides, and other success materials.

During his career, Hill founded three magazines: *Hill's Golden Rule* in 1919, *Napoleon Hill's Magazine* in 1921, and *Inspiration Magazine* in 1931. An ardent admirer of Orison Swett Marden, he revived *SUCCESS* magazine and served as its editor. In 1954, he joined with Stone to found *Success Unlimited* magazine.

Hill died on November 8, 1970, at his retirement home on Paris Mountain near Greenville, South Carolina.

The Napoleon Hill Foundation is a not-for-profit educational institution dedicated to making the world a better place in which to live.

Direct inquiries to:

University of Virginia/Wise

1 College Avenue, P.O. Box 1277

Wise, Virginia 24293

Phone: 276-328-6700 | Fax: 276-328-8752

Email: napoleonhill@uvawise.edu

Website: www.naphill.org

NEW! Only from Simple Truths®

spark impact in just one hour

IGNITE READS IS A NEW SERIES OF 1-HOUR READS WRITTEN BY WORLD-RENOWNED EXPERTS!

These captivating books will help you become the best version of yourself, allowing for new opportunities in your personal and professional life. Accelerate your career and expand your knowledge with these powerful books written on today's hottest ideas.

TRENDING BUSINESS AND PERSONAL GROWTH TOPICS

 Read in an hour or less

 Leading experts and authors

 Bold design and captivating content